7892

RL 6.1

A New True Book

NUCLEAR ENERGY

By Dennis B. Fradin

Consultant: Cary Davids, Ph.D.
Argonne National Laboratory
Argonne, Illinois

CHILDRENS PRESS ®

CHICAGO

Nuclear cooling tower in
Michigan City, Indiana

PHOTO CREDITS

AP/Wide World Photos, Inc.—19, 22, 31 (left), 32, 34
(left), 35 (2 photos)

© Cameramann International, Ltd—28, 31 (right), 37
(2 photos), 40 (2 photos), 41, 42

EKM-Nepenthe—34 (right)
© Robert Eckert—25 (left)
© James F. Pribble—25 (right)

Marilyn Gartman Agency: © Lee Baltermann—43

© Jerry Hennen—Cover

Journalism Services:
© Ingrid Johnsson—24
© Harvey Moshman—2
© John Patsch—11
© Harry J. Przekop—44 (top left and bottom)

Nawrocki Stock photo: © Jim Wright—4 (bottom)

Odyssey Productions, Chicago: © Robert Frerck—7
(left), 8, 44, (top right)

© Photri—14, 17, 20, (left), 26

© Th-Foto/Zefa/H. Armstrong Roberts—45

© Three Lions/Photo Source International—20 (right)

Tom Stack & Associates:
© David Doody—38 (2 photos)
© Brian Parker—7 (right)
© Tom Stack—12

Valan Photos: © M. Julien—4 (top)
—6, 9

Cover: Byron nuclear power station

Library of Congress Cataloging-in-Publication Data

Fradin, Dennis B.
  Nuclear energy.

  (A New true book)
  Includes index.
  Summary: Surveys the methods, history, advantages,
disadvantages, and future of nuclear energy.
    1. Nuclear energy—Juvenile literature.
[1. Nuclear energy] I. Title.
TK9148.F73 1987   333.79′24   86-31002
ISBN 0-516-01237-1

Childrens Press, Chicago
Copyright ©1987 by Regensteiner Publishing Enterprises, Inc.
All rights reserved. Published simultaneously in Canada.
Printed in the United States of America.
 ' 2 3 4 5 6 7 8 9 10 R 96 95 94 93 92 91 90 89 88

TABLE OF CONTENTS

Everything in the world is made of atoms. Scientists have been able to identify more than 100 of these basic elements in the universe.

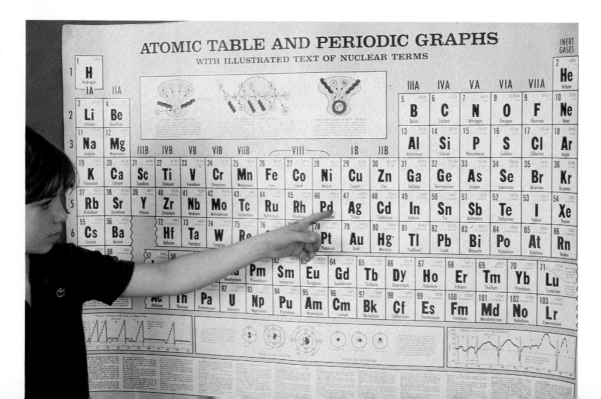

WHAT ARE ATOMS?

Atoms are tiny units that make up matter. Stars, people, and everything else we know are all made of atoms. Atoms are much too small to be seen by the human eye alone. In fact, many millions of atoms could fit on the period that ends this sentence.

Although atoms are tiny, they are huge compared to the particles inside them.

neutrons
protons
electrons

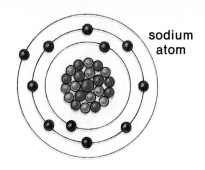
sodium atom

Three main kinds of
particles are found in
atoms. The three are
protons, neutrons, and
electrons.

Protons and neutrons are
in the center of an atom.
This central area is called
the *nucleus* (plural *nuclei*).
The electrons are outside
the nucleus and orbit the
nucleus billions of times
per second.

THE ELEMENTS

There are about 100 basic substances in the universe. These basic substances are called *elements*. Gold is an element. Iron, oxygen, hydrogen, and uranium are four others.

Miners (left) drill for gold (right) in a South African mine.

Scientists know that each atom of iron has 26 protons. An atom of gold has 79 protons.

Have you ever wondered what it is about gold that makes it gold? Or what it is about iron that makes it iron and *not* gold? During the early 1900s scientists learned the answer to such questions. The number of protons in an atom decides its identity.

No matter where it is—
whether in a glass of
water or inside a star—an
atom with just one proton
is hydrogen. An atom with
two protons has to be
helium. Gold differs from
iron because an iron atom
has 26 protons while a
gold atom has 79 protons.

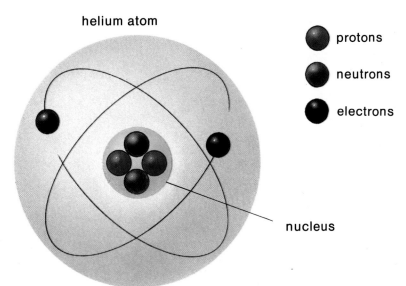

helium atom

protons

neutrons

electrons

nucleus

NUCLEAR ENERGY

Changes can occur in the structure of the nuclei of atoms. These changes are called *nuclear reactions*. In some nuclear reactions a great deal of energy escapes from the nuclei. Energy created in a nuclear reaction is called *nuclear energy*, or *atomic energy*.

Some nuclear energy is produced naturally. For

example, the Sun and
other stars make heat and
light by nuclear reactions.
People can manufacture
nuclear energy, too.

Nuclear power plant on the shores of Lake Michigan

Machines called *nuclear reactors* provide electricity for many cities. Man-made nuclear reactions are also used to explode atomic and hydrogen bombs.

PRODUCING NUCLEAR ENERGY

There are two ways that people produce nuclear energy. One way is called *nuclear fission.* The other is called *nuclear fusion.*

Fission means "splitting into pieces." In nuclear fission, the nuclei of atoms are split. This releases the energy from the nuclei. The atomic bomb and nuclear reactors work by fission.

Mushroom cloud caused by the nuclear bomb dropped
on Bikini Island on May 21, 1960

The element uranium is
the main fuel used to
create nuclear fission.
Uranium is good for this
for several reasons.
Uranium nuclei can be
split easily by shooting
neutrons at them. Also,

once a uranium nucleus is split, more neutrons are released which can split other uranium nuclei. This starts a *chain reaction*—an event which is a little like a row of dominoes knocking each other down.

Nuclear fusion is the other way to produce nuclear reactions. It occurs when nuclei of atoms join together, or fuse. This happens only under very hot conditions.

The Sun creates heat

and light by nuclear fusion. What happens in the Sun is that hydrogen nuclei fuse to make helium. In the process, matter is lost from the hydrogen nuclei. This lost matter is turned into heat and light.

Humanity's most powerful destructive weapon also works by fusion. It is called the *hydrogen bomb*. The explosion of an atomic bomb attached to the hydrogen bomb provides heat to start fusion.

An atomic bomb was used to explode this hydrogen bomb.

Hydrogen nuclei fuse to form helium, in much the same way as occurs in the Sun. As this happens, huge amounts of energy are released from the hydrogen nuclei, producing a huge explosion.

A SHORT HISTORY
OF NUCLEAR ENERGY

Our Sun has produced nuclear energy for about five billion years. People have been creating it for only about fifty years. The Nuclear Age began on December 2, 1942, at the University of Chicago. On that day a group led by the Italian-born scientist Enrico Fermi (1901–1954)

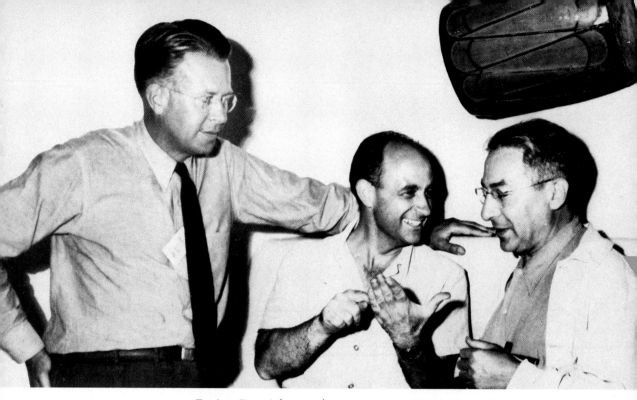

Enrico Fermi (center) chats with E.O. Lawrence (left) and Isidor L. Rabi (right) at Los Alamos National Laboratory in New Mexico.

made a chain reaction in a pile of uranium.

World War II was raging at the time. The United States used the knowledge gathered by Fermi and others to build atomic

On August 6, 1945 the atomic bomb (left) destroyed the city of Hiroshima, Japan and killed over 100,000 people.

bombs. On August 6, 1945, the United States dropped an atomic bomb on Hiroshima, Japan. The temperature at the explosion point reached ninety million degrees Fahrenheit (fifty million degrees Celsius)—hotter than the Sun's core. About 100,000 people died during or soon after the blast.

Three days later, the United States dropped an atomic bomb on Nagasaki, Japan. This bomb killed about 40,000 people right away. The United States dropped those two atomic bombs on Japan to help end World War II. But many people thought it

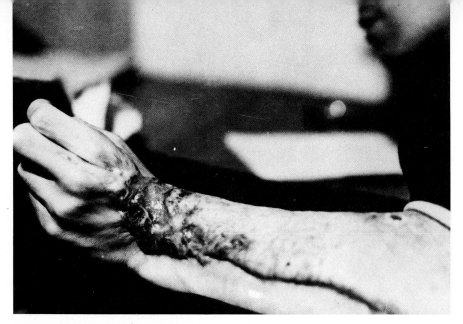
Severe burn caused by the atomic bomb explosion

was wrong to bring about so much death and destruction.

A few years later, a bomb thousands of times more powerful than the atomic bomb was built. This new weapon was the *hydrogen bomb*. The first

large hydrogen bomb was
exploded on November 1,
1952, by the United States.
During the next few years
the United States, Russia,
and several other nations
exploded hundreds of
hydrogen and atomic
bombs. These blasts were
all tests. No bombs were
dropped on people.
Nuclear bombs are still
being tested. Most of these
tests are now done
underground.

During the 1950s, people also found peaceful uses for nuclear energy. The main peaceful use was in nuclear power plants which produced electricity. The first major nuclear power plant opened in England in 1956. During the next few years, many other nations

Nuclear plant in France

Trojan Nuclear Power Plant in Oregon (left) and
the Prairie Island Nuclear Power Plant in Minnesota (right)

built nuclear power plants.
Today there are about
400 nuclear power plants
in the world. They generate
approximately one-sixth of
the world's electric power.
The United States has
more nuclear power plants
than any other country—
about 100 of them.

Ratcliffe
Nuclear Power
Plant in
Great Britain

THE ADVANTAGES
OF NUCLEAR ENERGY

Nuclear energy has
helped humanity in several
big ways. For one thing,
Earth has limited supplies
of coal and oil, the fuels
most non-nuclear plants

use to produce electricity. Nuclear power plants do not rely on coal or oil. If coal and oil become scarce, nuclear power plants could still produce electricity.

Second, nuclear power plants need less fuel than do coal- or oil-burning plants. One ton of uranium produces more energy than is produced by several million tons of coal or several million barrels of oil.

The control room at a nuclear power station is
run by highly skilled and specially trained workers.

Third, coal- and oil-
burning plants dirty the air.
Coal especially pollutes the
air. Nuclear reactors do not
release pollution—if they
are working right.

THE DISADVANTAGES OF NUCLEAR ENERGY

The nations of the world now have enough nuclear bombs to kill every person on Earth several times. The two strongest nations— Russia and the United States—have about 50,000 nuclear weapons between them. What if there were to be a nuclear war? Or what if nuclear weapons were launched by accident?

Nuclear explosions produce energy in the form of heat, light, and *nuclear radiation*. Materials produced during the explosion are capable of giving off nuclear radiation. When these materials fall back to Earth they are called *fallout*. The nuclear radiation in fallout harms the cells of the human body. Depending on the dose, fallout can make people sick or even kill them.

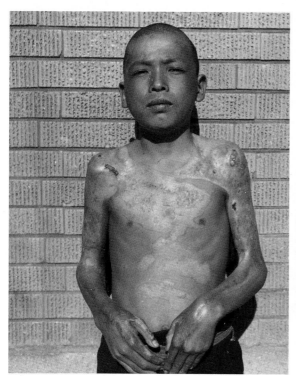

Radiation burns (left) and illnesses caused by radiation killed people in Japan years after the 1945 blast. Each year a festival honoring the dead is held in Hiroshima in front of the only building left standing after the A-bomb fell.

Illness can strike people years after their exposure to nuclear radiation. Due to radiation they received in 1945, thousands of people

31

In order to limit dangerous fallout, most nuclear bomb tests are underground.

in Hiroshima and Nagasaki
developed cancer years
later. Hundreds of
American citizens have
also died from the effects
of fallout produced in
nuclear tests.

Nuclear reactors can be

dangerous, too. One reactor disaster is called a *meltdown*. This is an accident in which uranium fuel melts, releasing large amounts of radiation. In 1979 the cooling system failed at the Three Mile Island nuclear reactor near Harrisburg, Pennsylvania. Radiation leaked, forcing tens of thousands of people to flee. The problem was solved minutes before a total meltdown would have

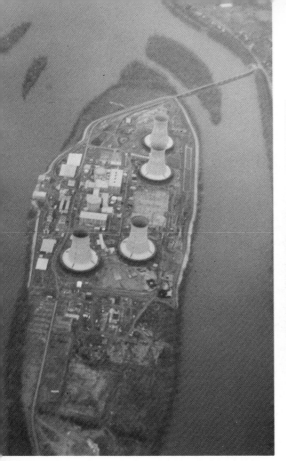

Two views of Three Mile Island

occurred. Fortunately, no
deaths occurred as a
result of this accident.

A much worse disaster
struck Russia's Chernobyl
Nuclear Power Plant in

After the Chernobyl disaster, special solutions (left) were used to wash down people, clothes, and equipment that were exposed to radioactive fallout. Medical technician (right) checks a mother and her child for dangerous radiation levels.

spring of 1986. This time a great deal of radiation leaked. Hundreds of thousands of Russians and people living nearby in Eastern Europe were exposed to the radiation. Several dozen people near the power plant died within a few days. At some time in the future, thousands more may die of cancer caused by the radiation they received in 1986.

Nuclear reactors also have waste disposal problems. Reactors produce nuclear waste products. These wastes emit dangerous radiation, in some cases the danger is expected to last for thousands of years. Because they could kill

Spent fuel rods (left) are
enclosed in cylinders. Others are
stored under water (right).

people who touch them,
even in future years,
nuclear wastes cannot be
thrown away like ordinary
garbage. Currently many
nuclear wastes are stored

Workers at nuclear power plants regularly check radiation levels.

in special pools at the
nuclear reactors. The
United States plans to
move its nuclear wastes to
a remote underground
dump during the late
1990s. The plan calls for

the dump to be carefully guarded and maintained.

An accident which happened in 1957 shows how important it is to carefully store nuclear wastes. It happened at a dump site in Russia's Ural Mountains, several hundred miles east of Moscow. Buried nuclear wastes mysteriously exploded. Russia gave no details about this disaster, but dozens of people are thought to have died.

Control room (above) operates the nuclear fusion reactor
at a Japanese research institute. Aerial view of the Dresden
Nuclear Power Station (below) in Morris, Illinois.

There is one more
problem with nuclear
reactors. They last only
about fifty years. Some day
the nuclear power plants in
use now will have to be
replaced by new ones. The
old plants will have plenty
of radiation locked inside

Each building houses a nuclear reactor.

Spent fuel cask sits on a railroad car outside a nuclear storage facility.

them. They may have to
be covered by concrete
and guarded for thousands
of years. Or perhaps they
will be taken apart and
buried in places where no
one will be permitted to
dig.

Nuclear power plant in Byron, Illinois

THE FUTURE OF NUCLEAR ENERGY

Ever since nuclear energy was first used, people have argued about it. Lawmakers, scientists, and ordinary citizens are still arguing about it. Some

43

Every effort is made to protect people from harmful radiation. Lead containers (above) are used to transport radioactive materials. Warning signs (right) are posted when radioactive materials are present. Strict government inspections oversee all new nuclear power plant constructions.

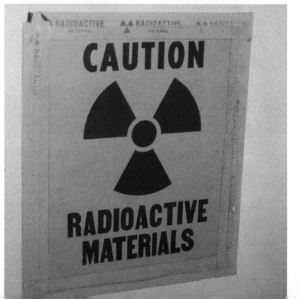

people think that nuclear
energy is here to stay and
that we must learn to live
with it. Others say that we
should get rid of all
nuclear weapons and
power plants. Still others
have opinions that fall
somewhere in between.

What do you think?

WORDS YOU SHOULD KNOW

atom(AT • um) — very tiny units that make up an element of matter

atomic bomb(uh • TOM • ik BAHMB) — a powerful bomb which works by nuclear fission

cancer(KAN • sir) — a disease in which cells multiply wildly

chain reaction(CHANE ree • AK • shun) — a process which keeps going by itself

electron(ih • LEK • trahn) — a particle which orbits an atom's nucleus and which has a negative electric charge

elements(EL • ih • ments) — the basic substances in the universe

fallout(FAWL • out) — harmful radiation that falls to Earth following a nuclear explosion

hydrogen(HI • drih • gin) — an element which has one proton in each of its atoms

hydrogen bomb(HI • drih • gin) — a nuclear fusion bomb which is the most powerful weapon ever built

matter(MAT • er) — the substance of which physical objects are made up

meltdown(MELT • down) — an accident in which the uranium fuel in a nuclear reactor melts, releasing tremendous amounts of radiation

million(MIL • yun) — a thousand thousand (1,000,000)

molecule(MAHL • ih • kyool) — tiny particle of matter made up of one or more atoms

neutron(NOO • trahn) — a particle which is found in an atom's nucleus and which has no electric charge

nuclear energy(NOO • klee • er EN • er • gee) — the energy produced by changes in the nuclei of atoms

nuclear fission(NOO • klee • er FISH • un) — a process in which nuclei of atoms are split, releasing tremendous energy

nuclear fusion(NOO •klee •er FYOO •zjun)—a process in which nuclei of atoms join together, releasing tremendous energy

nuclear power plants(NOO •klee •er POW •er PLANTS)— buildings where electricity is produced from nuclear energy

nuclear radiation(NOO •klee •er ray •dee •A •shun)—the energy given off by the nuclei of atoms in the form of waves or particles

nuclear reaction(NOO •klee •er re •AK •shun)—an event, sometimes accompanied by the release of energy, in which changes occur in the nuclei of atoms

nuclear reactors(NOO •klee •er re •AK •terz)—machines which split atomic nuclei to produce electricity

nuclear weapons(NOO •klee •er WEP •unz)—atomic bombs, hydrogen bombs, and all other weapons which draw their power from the release of atomic energy

nuclei(NOO •klee •eye)—plural of nucleus

nucleus (of an atom)(NOO •klee •uss)—the center of the atom where the protons and neutrons are located

particle (of matter)(PAR •tik •ihl)—one of the tiny subdivisions of matter (atom or molecule)

pollution(puh •LOO •shun)—the dirtying of the air, water, and soil

proton(PRO •tahn)—a particle which is found in the nucleus of an atom and which has a positive electric charge

ton(TUN)—two thousand (2,000) pounds

uranium(yoo •RAY •nee •um)—an element which is the main fuel used to create nuclear fission

INDEX

About the author

Dennis Fradin attended Northwestern University on a partial creative scholarship and was graduated in 1967. His previous books include the Young People's Stories of Our States series for Childrens Press, and Bad Luck Tony for Prentice-Hall. In the True book series Dennis has written about astronomy, farming, comets, archaeology, movies, space colonies, the space lab, explorers, and pioneers. He is married and the father of three children.